B1 Listening

Ten practice tests for the **Cambridge B1 Preliminary**

Anna Phillips and Terry Phillips

PROSPERITY EDUCATION

© Prosperity Education Ltd. 2025

Registered offices: Sherlock Close, Cambridge
CB3 0HP, United Kingdom

First published 2025; Revised edition: 2026

ISBN: 978-1-915654-47-2

Original edition © Innova Content Ltd.

This publication is in copyright. Subject to statutory exception and to the provisions of relevant collective licensing agreements, no reproduction of any part may take place without the written permission of Prosperity Education.

This edition is published by arrangement with Innova Content Ltd.

The moral rights of the authors have been asserted.

'Cambridge B1 Preliminary' and 'PET' are brands belonging to The Chancellor, Masters and Scholars of the University of Cambridge and are not associated with Prosperity Education or its products.

Designed by ORP Cambridge

Audio production by Wired Studios Ltd.

For further information and resources, visit:
www.prosperityeducation.net

To infinity and beyond.

Contents

Introduction *v*

Test 1 *1*

Test 2 *9*

Test 3 *17*

Test 4 *25*

Test 5 *33*

Test 6 *41*

Test 7 *49*

Test 8 *57*

Test 9 *65*

Test 10 *73*

Answers *81*

How to download the audio and transcripts

1. Go to www.prosperityeducation.net
2. Select the Downloads page
3. Select the book cover image
4. Password: **TIAB**
5. Download the audio .mp3 content
6. Download the transcript .pdf content

A digital platform for Cambridge exam preparation

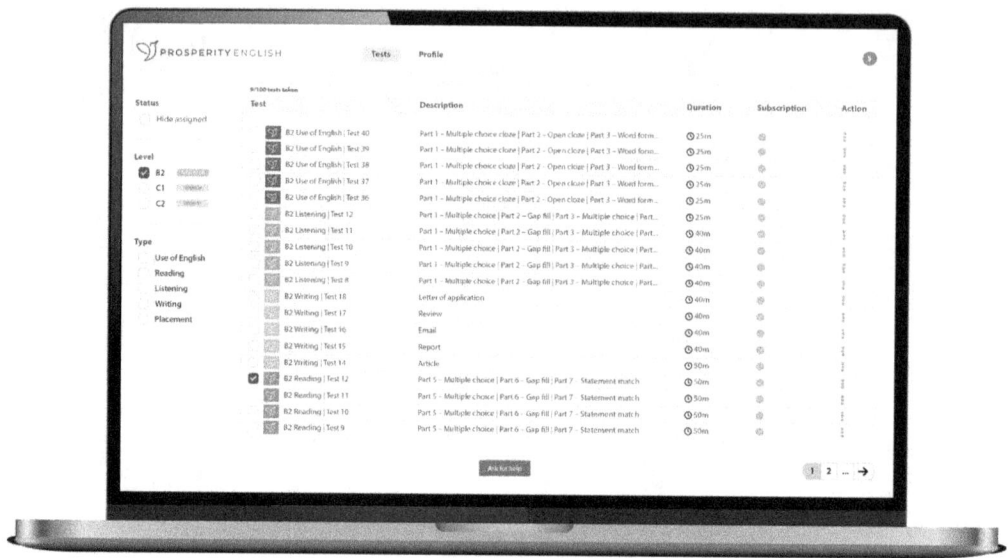

Prosperity English provides ample opportunities for repetitive practice, allowing you to reinforce your learning and improve your exam skills steadily.

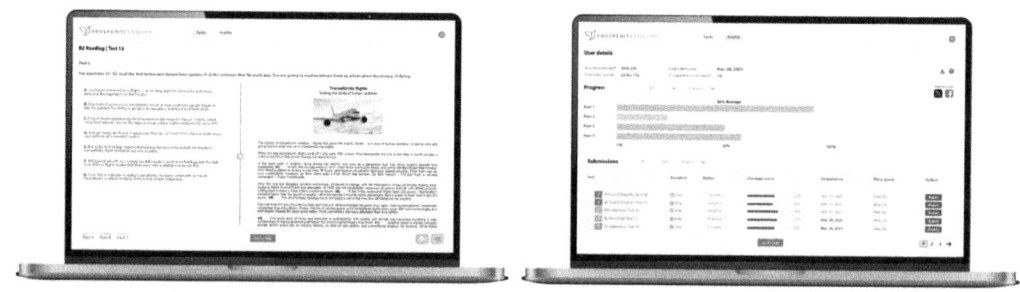

Try it for free

www.prosperityenglish.com

40% promotional discount code:
TIAB40

Introduction

Welcome to this edition of sample tests for the Cambridge B1 Preliminary Listening, which has been written to replicate the Cambridge exam experience and has undergone rigorous expert and peer review.

The B1 Preliminary English language exam is the third of six levels established in the Common European Framework of Reference (CEFR): A1–C2. Candidates of all ages can take the B1 Preliminary test. In the exam you will have 30 minutes to complete the Listening paper. This section has four parts, and is worth 25% of the final score.

The Listening section of the examination tests candidates' abilities to follow a diverse range of spoken English, and to understand the speakers' personal opinions and attitudes, specific information being conveyed and also the general meaning of lengthier monologues. It is broken down into four parts.

	Number of questions	Number of marks	Task types	What do candidates have to do?
Part 1	7	7	3-option multiple choice	Identify key information in seven short monologues or dialogues and choose the correct visual.
Part 2	6	6	3-option multiple choice	Listen to six short dialogues and understand the gist of each.
Part 3	6	6	Gap fill	Listen to a monologue and complete six gaps.
Part 4	6	6	3-option multiple choice	Listen to an interview for a detailed understanding of meaning and to identify attitudes and opinions.
Total	25	25		

For more information, visit the Cambridge Assessment English website.

This book contains 10 Listening tests (Parts 1–4), comprising a total of 250 individual assessments. You or your students, if you are a teacher, will hopefully enjoy the wide range of texts and benefit from the repetitive practice, something that is key to preparing for this part of the B1 Preliminary (PET) examination.

We hope that you will find this resource a useful study aid, and wish you all the best in preparing for the exam.

Cambridge B1 Preliminary

Listening

Test 1

© 2025 Prosperity Education.
'Cambridge B1 Preliminary' and 'PET' are brands belonging to The Chancellor, Masters and Scholars of the University of Cambridge and are not associated with Prosperity Education or its products.

Part 1

Questions 1 – 7

For each question, choose the correct answer.

---

1 What does Amelia want to do this weekend?

   A   B   C

2 What did the boy watch on television last night?

   A   B   C

3 What do the children need to get first?

   A   B   C

4 Where did the accident happen?

A

B

C

5 How does the girl usually get to school?

A

B

C

6 Which story does the girl prefer?

A

B

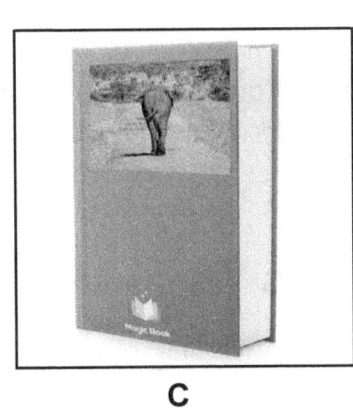
C

7 What did the boy hurt at the hockey game?

A

B

C

Turn over ▶

Part 2

Questions 8 – 13

For each question, choose the correct answer.

---

8 You will hear two friends talking about a film they have seen.
What did the girl like best about it?

    A It was a love story.

    B It was about a girl her age.

    C The boy and the girl finally met each other.

9 You will hear two friends talking about next term.
The boy wants to study

    A the three sciences.

    B biology, history and English.

    C biology, history and geography.

10 You will hear a boy telling his friend about his skiing holiday.
How did he feel about skiing?

    A It was good to do once.

    B He really enjoyed it in the end.

    C He didn't like the experience at all.

11 You will hear two friends talking about learning to play chess.
The girl advises the boy

    A to play more games.

    B not to make the same mistakes each time.

    C to defend rather than attack at the beginning.

12 You will hear two friends talking about a museum they've been to.
They agree about

    A   the best items in the museum.

    B   the way you seemed to walk through time as you went round.

    C   the organisation of the museum.

13 You will hear two friends talking about a meal they've had.
They agree that

    A   the service was poor.

    B   the food was good.

    C   the restaurant was expensive.

Turn over ▶

Part 3

Questions 14 – 19

For each question, write the correct answer in the gap. Write **one** or **two words** or a **number** or a **date** or a **time**.

You will hear a man called Henry Brooks telling a group of students about his work as writer.

Being a writer
Henry wrote a play when he was **(14)** ....
Henry doesn't get his ideas from his **(15)** ....
Henry's first published work was a **(16)** ....
Henry was paid £ **(17)** .... for his first published work
At that time, he was a **(18)** ....
Next year, Henry will start to write for **(19)** ....

Part 4

Questions 20 – 25

For each question, choose the correct answer.

You will hear a radio interview with a young actor called Ellen.

20 The first part Ellen remembers playing is

- A a donkey.
- B a queen.
- C a dog.

21 What first attracted Ellen to acting?

- A dressing up
- B playing parts like a queen
- C making people laugh and cry

22 Why does Ellen say she's an 'actor'?

- A She thinks it is an old word.
- B She thinks people pay actresses less than actors.
- C She doesn't believe in differences between people in the same job.

23 When did she make the decision to go to drama school?

- A at 15
- B at 16
- C at 18

24 How did her mother react to her decision?

- A She supported it.
- B She didn't say anything about it.
- C She didn't want her to go.

25 In her future career, Ellen wants to

- A stay where she is and do more plays.
- B visit Los Angeles.
- C work in films.

Cambridge B1 Preliminary

Listening

Test 2

Listening B1 | Ten tests for the Cambridge Preliminary

Part 1

Questions 1 – 7

For each question, choose the correct answer.

---

1 What does the boy usually do first in the evenings

A

B

C

2 What is the girl's favourite subject at school?

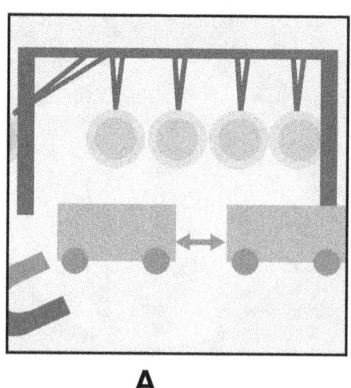
A

B

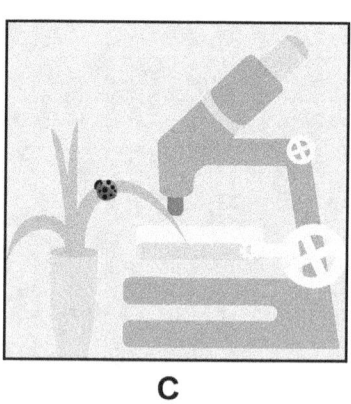
C

3 What are the children going to see first?

A

B

C

4 Where did the police find the boat?

A

B

C

5 What is the girl learning about in geography this term?

A

B

C

6 Which part of the water park did the girl like best?

A

B

C

7 Who does the boy have to visit in hospital?

A

B

C

Turn over ▶

Part 2

Questions 8 – 13

For each question, choose the correct answer.

---

8   You will hear two friends talking about a book they have read.
    What did the girl like best about it?

    A   It was very funny.

    B   She couldn't guess the ending.

    C   It made her think about society.

9   You will hear two friends talking about their weekend jobs.
    What does the girl do?

    A   She delivers newspapers.

    B   She fills up the shelves.

    C   She takes money from people.

10 You will hear a boy telling his friend about an accident.
    Why did the accident happen?

    A   His mother shouted at him.

    B   His little brother tripped him up.

    C   He fell over the cat.

11 You will hear two friends talking about driving lessons.
    The girl advises the boy

    A   to focus on one point in each lesson.

    B   to stay calm when he makes mistakes.

    C   to have more than one lesson a week.

12 You will hear two friends talking about a concert they have been to.
They agree about

    A   the band's later songs.

    B   the band's early songs.

    C   the lead guitarist.

13 You will hear two friends talking about their school uniform.
They agree that

    A   school uniforms are a good idea.

    B   their own uniforms are not good.

    C   people shouldn't wear expensive clothes to school.

Turn over ▶

Part 3

Questions 14 – 19

For each question, write the correct answer in the gap. Write **one** or **two words** or a **number** or a **date** or a **time**.

You will hear a woman called Millie Green telling a group of students about her work as a photographer.

Being a photographer

Millie particularly likes photographing **(14)** ....

Millie took her first photograph at **(15)** ....

Millie thinks expensive film taught people to think about the **(16)** .... of a photograph.

Millie's course cost over £ **(17)** ....

Millie says you must learn the **(18)** .... of a job.

Millie hates photographing **(19)** ....

Part 4

Questions 20 – 25

For each question, choose the correct answer.

You will hear a radio interview with a young man called Mark.

20 Mark prefers to be called

    A   a house husband.
    B   a home maker.
    C   by his first name.

21 Who works in Mark's family?

    A   Both he and his wife work.
    B   His wife works and he doesn't.
    C   He works and his wife doesn't.

22 What does Mark think about what he does?

    A   He should get money from the government for the work.
    B   The government should pay men when they look after children.
    C   Looking after children is a very important job.

23 How does Mark feel about managers getting paid more than teachers?

    A   He thinks they should be paid the same.
    B   He thinks they deserve the extra money.
    C   He think teachers should earn more than managers.

24 What did Mark and his wife expect to happen after she had their first child?

    A   She would look after the baby and Mark would continue to work.
    B   Someone else would look after the baby and they would both go back to work.
    C   Mark would stop work and his wife would continue to work.

25 In the future, Mark will

    A   go back to teaching.
    B   get a job in charge of education in the area.
    C   continue to be responsible for the children, the cooking and the house.

Cambridge B1 Preliminary

Listening

Test 3

© 2025 Prosperity Education.
'Cambridge B1 Preliminary' and 'PET' are brands belonging to The Chancellor, Masters and Scholars of the University of Cambridge and are not associated with Prosperity Education or its products.

Listening B1 | Ten tests for the Cambridge Preliminary

Part 1

Questions 1 – 7

For each question, choose the correct picture.

---

1   Where does the girl want to go on Saturday?

A

B

C

2   What did the boy have to eat at the restaurant last night?

A

B

C

3   What must the students bring on the school trip?

A

B

C

4 Where was the dog found?

A B C

5 How did the girl spend her summer holiday?

A B C

6 What did the girl like the most at the robot exhibition?

A B C

7 Who does the boy have to see after school today?

A B C

Turn over ▶

Part 2

Questions 8 – 13

For each question, choose the correct answer.

---

8   You will hear two friends talking about a film they have seen.
    What didn't the girl like about it?

    A   the actor playing the man

    B   the actor playing the woman

    C   the story

9   You will hear two friends talking about their school subjects.
    What is the girl going to do?

    A   stop taking geography

    B   stop studying history

    C   continue with both history and geography

10 You will hear a boy telling his friend about a birthday present.
    What did he get?

    A   a very big television

    B   a bicycle

    C   a computer

11 You will hear two friends talking about after-school clubs.
    The girl advises the boy

    A   not to go to the football and chess clubs.

    B   to go to four clubs.

    C   to go to the drama club instead of the chess club.

12 You will hear two friends talking about a play they have been to.
They agree about

    A   the ending.

    B   the acting.

    C   the costumes.

13 You will hear two friends talking about a football match.
They agree that

    A   both teams played well.

    B   the winning team was lucky.

    C   the result was fair.

Turn over ▶

Part 3

Questions 14 – 19

For each question, write the correct answer in the gap. Write **one** or **two words** or a **number** or a **date** or a **time**.

You will hear a university student called Chris Jones talking to a group of school students.

Studying at university

Chris left the school **(14)** .... months ago.

Chris says university will be good if you follow his **(15)** ....

People won't **(16)** .... you about things like work and food and sleep.

If the university work is hard for you, **(17)** .... about it.

You have to learn how to **(18)** ....

After a lecture, you have to do **(19)** ....

Part 4

Questions 20 – 25

For each question, choose the correct answer.

You will hear a radio interview with a young gymnast called Jenny.

20 Jenny has been a gymnast

   A   for fourteen and a half years.
   B   since she was 5.
   C   from the age of 3.

21 Why does Jenny remember her first performance?

   A   She saw the effect it had on the audience.
   B   It was with a ball and a ribbon.
   C   She made several mistakes during the performance.

22 Why is it harder being a gymnast now than when she was younger?

   A   She doesn't have a social life at the weekend.
   B   She has schoolwork as well as training and performances.
   C   She has to train for longer now each day.

23 How many areas has Jenny won competitions in?

   A   three
   B   four
   C   six

24 Jenny is allowed to compete in the next Olympics because

   A   she is over 14.
   B   they have changed the rules.
   C   she will be over 16 in the year before the Games.

25 At the next Olympic Games, Jenny thinks she might win

   A   three individual medals.
   B   four individual medals.
   C   five individual medals.

Cambridge B1 Preliminary

Listening

Test 4

Part 1

Questions 1 – 7

For each question, choose the correct answer.

1   Where did the boy meet his friends yesterday?

A

B

C

2   Why did the girl's mother get ill?

A

B

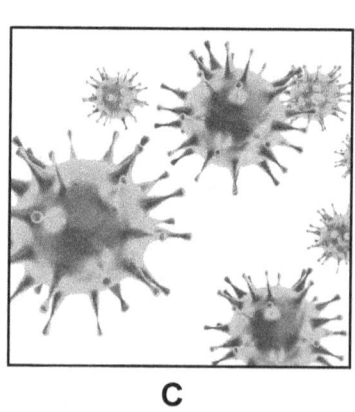
C

3   What does the experiment start with?

A

B

C

4 What happened at the music festival this year?

A

B

C

5 How did the girl get to school today?

A

B

C

6 What did the girl like the most at Nature World?

A

B

C

7 What is the boy going to play this afternoon?

A

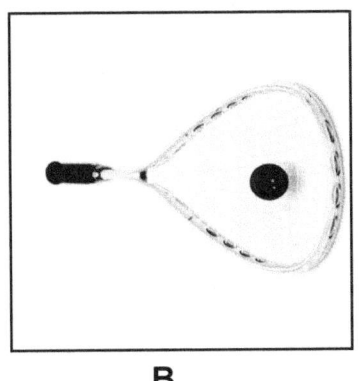
B

C

Turn over ▶

Part 2

Questions 8 – 13

For each question, choose the correct answer.

---

8   You will hear two friends talking about a book they have read.
    What did the girl like best about it?

    A   the length of the book

    B   the ending of the story

    C   the development of the characters

9   You will hear two friends talking about clothes.
    What has the girl just bought?

    A   a dress

    B   a hat

    C   shoes

10   You will hear a boy telling his friend about a football match.
     What was the final score?

    A   1-0 to the boy's team

    B   2-1 to the other team

    C   2-2

11   You will hear two friends talking about the weather.
     The girl advises the boy

    A   to go home immediately.

    B   to catch the school bus.

    C   to call his mother for a lift.

12 You will hear two friends talking about an after-school club.
They agree that

    A   the Art Club is better than the art lessons.

    B   animals are a good subject for painting.

    C   the final activity is useful.

13 You will hear two friends talking about music.
They agree that

    A   songs are better than music without words.

    B   the Polar Bears pop group are good.

    C   rap music is clever.

Turn over ▶

Part 3

Questions 14 – 19

For each question, write the correct answer in the gap. Write **one** or **two words** or a **number** or a **date** or a **time**.

You will hear a man called Paul Brooks talking to a group of school students about getting a good job.

Getting a good job

You should be interested in this talk even if you are only **(14)** ....

An employer must **(15)** .... to employ you.

It is possible that you will have **(16)** .... jobs in different areas.

Most employers need people with good **(17)** .... skills.

Try to be more **(18)** .... by using planners.

Become an expert at the basic computer **(19)** ....

Part 4

Questions 20 – 25

For each question, choose the correct answer.

You will hear a radio interview with a young scientist called Lucy.

20 Lucy started doing experiments

  A at school.
  B when she was nine.
  C when her parents got a shed.

21 Where did Lucy get things for her experiments from at first?

  A the kitchen
  B a chemistry set
  C school

22 For the experiment that exploded, Lucy got the instructions from

  A her mother.
  B school.
  C the internet.

23 Why wasn't Lucy's mother angry about the experiment?

  A Similar things had happened to her.
  B She was a chemist.
  C Lucy wasn't hurt.

24 Why did Lucy become a chemist?

  A because her mother was a chemist
  B because she liked seeing how things changed in experiments
  C she was inspired by the chemistry teacher at school.

25 In the future, Lucy believes medicines will stop

  A all cancers from starting and growing.
  B a few cancers from starting and growing.
  C the majority of cancers from starting and growing.

Cambridge B1 Preliminary

Listening

Test 5

Listening B1 | Ten tests for the Cambridge Preliminary

Part 1

Questions 1 – 7

For each question, choose the correct answer.

---

1 Where does the girl want to go for the next summer holiday?

        A   B   C

2 What did the boy watch on television last night?

A   B   

                                                                             C

3 What must the athletes get first on sports day?

A   B   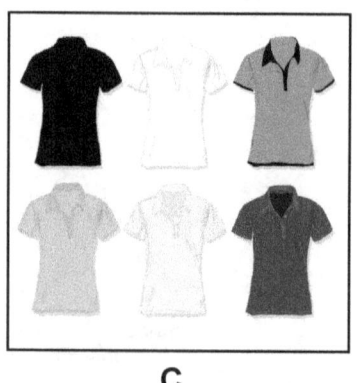

                                                                             C

4 Where did the fire officers find the car?

A

B

C

5 What does the girl usually have for lunch?

A

B

C

6 Which computer game did the girl like best?

A

B

C

7 What did the boy hurt during the football game?

A

B

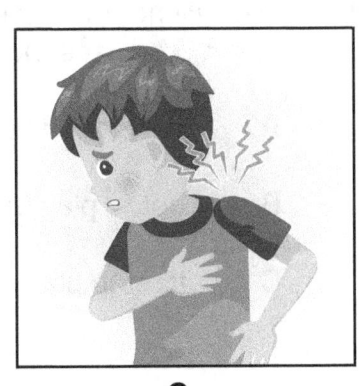
C

Turn over ▶

Part 2

Questions 8 – 13

For each question, choose the correct answer.

---

8   You will hear two friends talking about a science museum they have visited.
    What did the girl like best about it?

    A   the dinosaur in the main hall

    B   the wildlife photographs

    C   the bones in the last room

9   You will hear two friends talking about next year.
    What subjects does the girl want to do?

    A   English, history and maths

    B   physics, chemistry and maths

    C   physics, chemistry and biology

10 You will hear a boy telling his friend about a music festival.
    Why was the festival stopped?

    A   The lights went out.

    B   The wind was too strong.

    C   The field became flooded.

11 You will hear two friends talking about tennis lessons.
    The girl advises the boy

    A   to work on each skill on his own.

    B   not to play any more games for a while.

    C   to stop playing tennis.

12 You will hear two friends talking about a story they have read.
They agree that the story

   A   is stupid.

   B   is not really fiction.

   C   suggests a possible future world.

13 You will hear two friends talking about a meal they've had.
They agree that

   A   it was a very big meal.

   B   you shouldn't send things back to the kitchen.

   C   the chicken was better than the steak.

Turn over ▶

Part 3

Questions 14 – 19

For each question, write the correct answer in the gap. Write **one** or **two words** or a **number** or a **date** or a **time**.

You will hear a man called James Grant telling a group of students about his work as an architect.

Being an architect

James says he started his architecture career when he was **(14)** ....

He designed his first house for **(15)** ....

He learnt that architects must make the best use of **(16)** .... that is available.

He also learnt that architects must discover what their customers **(17)** ....

James says architects have to study at university for **(18)** .... years.

Architects learn about good design and about different **(19)** ....

Part 4

Questions 20 – 25

For each question, choose the correct answer.

You will hear a radio interview with a young drama teacher called Scarlet.

20 Scarlet says that

- **A** drama teachers are failed actors.
- **B** drama teachers don't want to be actors.
- **C** she never wanted to be an actor.

21 How is acting different from drama lessons?

- **A** You're watched by people you know in drama lessons.
- **B** Nobody watches you in drama lessons.
- **C** Most people who watch you in drama lessons are strangers.

22 When did Scarlet decide to become a drama teacher?

- **A** after a careers fair at her school
- **B** after speaking to her parents about possible careers
- **C** when she saw information from a training college

23 Why did Scarlet's father think it was a good choice?

- **A** Drama teachers are well-paid.
- **B** Scarlet would not have to change jobs many times.
- **C** Scarlet would be very good at it.

24 How did Scarlet get her present job?

- **A** The previous drama teacher retired.
- **B** She replaced someone who was having a baby.
- **C** A temporary job at a school became a permanent one.

25 Scarlet loves

- **A** seeing the development of acting skills.
- **B** putting children into real-life situations.
- **C** building up a child's ability to deal with the world.

Cambridge B1 Preliminary

Listening

Test 6

© 2025 Prosperity Education.
'Cambridge B1 Preliminary' and 'PET' are brands belonging to The Chancellor, Masters and Scholars of the University of Cambridge and are not associated with Prosperity Education or its products.

Part 1

Questions 1 – 7

For each question, choose the correct answer.

---

1 Where will Amy go on Sunday?

A

B

C

2 What did the boy see on television last night?

A

B

C

3 What must the children do first?

A

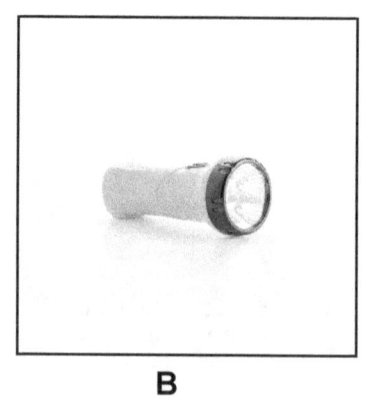
B

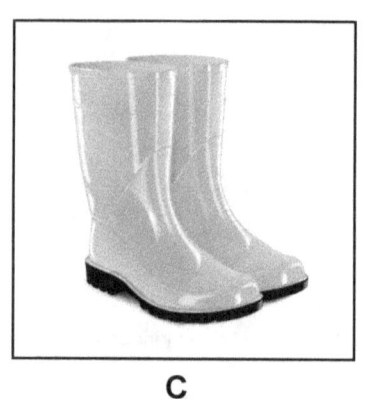
C

4 What was seen in some back gardens of Kingsland?

A

B

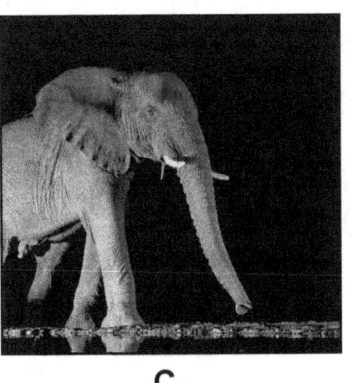
C

5 How does the girl usually get home?

A

B

C

6 Which poem did the girl prefer?

A

B

C

7 Where did the boy's father get hurt?

A

B

C

Turn over ▶

Part 2

Questions 8 – 13

For each question, choose the correct answer.

---

8   You will hear two friends talking about a film they have seen.
    What did the girl like best about it?

    A   the music

    B   the story

    C   the character development

9   You will hear two friends talking about next term.
    Which subjects will the boy take an exam in?

    A   maths, physics and chemistry

    B   maths and physics

    C   physics and chemistry

10 You will hear a boy telling his friend about his holiday.
    How does he feel about the holiday?

    A   He enjoyed it but felt it was too long.

    B   It was enjoyable despite the length of the days and the temperature.

    C   It was good to do once.

11 You will hear two friends talking about playing in a concert.
    The girl advises the boy

    A   to play the piece a lot more times on his own.

    B   to choose an easier piece.

    C   to try playing the piece for a small number of people.

12 You will hear two friends talking about an art gallery they've been to.
They agree that

    A   there wasn't enough variety of subject.

    B   there weren't enough paintings.

    C   the tickets were too expensive.

13 You will hear two friends talking about a meal they have had.
They agree that

    A   the waiter was not polite.

    B   the meat was good.

    C   the steak was cooked well for each of them.

Turn over ▶

Part 3

Questions 14 – 19

For each question, write the correct answer in the gap. Write **one** or **two words** or a **number** or a **date** or a **time**.

You will hear a man called Winston Fraser telling a group of students about his work as computer programmer.

Being a computer programmer
Winston started reading computer magazines at about **(14)** ....
Winston says computer language or code is like **(15)** ....
Early programs marked your typing mistakes with the word **(16)** ....
Winston didn't go to college because he already had **(17)** ....
Winston's first program was for language schools to record students' **(18)** ....
Winston thinks that one day in the future, we might not need **(19)** ....

Part 4

Questions 20 – 25

For each question, choose the correct answer.

You will hear a radio interview with a young police officer called Rose

20 Rose became a full-time police officer

    A   after studying law at university.
    B   after working as an unpaid officer.
    C   when she left school.

21 How many hours a week did Rose work as a Special Constable?

    A   4
    B   8
    C   8 to 10

22 What do Special Constables do before they start doing police work?

    A   attend training courses
    B   go with trained officers in police cars
    C   do a lot of office work

23 What can a Special Constable do?

    A   protect people in town centres help
    B   in emergency situations anything
    C   that a police officer can do

24 What does Rose think about the Special Constable idea?

    A   It's unfair because you don't get paid.
    B   It's a good way to find out if the job is right for you.
    C   It leads to a lot of people giving up becoming a police officer.

25 In the future, Rose wants to

    A   become a Detective Inspector.
    B   stay in uniform.
    C   continue with day to day police work.

Cambridge B1 Preliminary

Listening

Test 7

© 2025 Prosperity Education.
'Cambridge B1 Preliminary' and 'PET' are brands belonging to The Chancellor, Masters and Scholars of the University of Cambridge and are not associated with Prosperity Education or its products.

Listening B1 | Ten tests for the Cambridge Preliminary

Part 1

Questions 1 – 7

For each question, choose the correct answer.

---

1 Where does the boy usually go on Saturdays?

A

B

C

2 What is the girl doing instead of history next term?

A

B

C

3 Which item must the children deal with first?

A

B

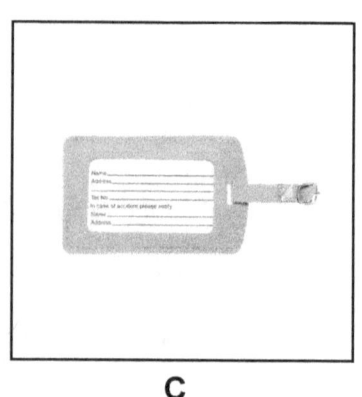
C

4 Where did the police find the animal?

A

B

C

5 What is the girl learning about in science this week?

A

B

C

6 Which part of the school trip did the girl like best?

A

B

C

7 How did the boy hurt his hand?

A

B

C

Turn over ▶

Part 2

Questions 8 – 13

For each question, choose the correct answer.

---

8 You will hear two friends talking about a book they have read. What did the girl like best about it?

    A   the explanation of the hero's actions

    B   the ending

    C   the heroine

9 You will hear two friends talking about after-school clubs. Which one does the girl go to regularly?

    A   Art Club

    B   Drama Club

    C   Music Club

10 You will hear a boy telling his friend about a problem. Why couldn't he go to school the day before?

    A   He couldn't get a lift from his father.

    B   He had to look after his mother.

    C   He had to go to the doctor.

11 You will hear two friends talking about tennis lessons. The girl advises the boy

    A   to watch the ball more.

    B   to try to win more points.

    C   to return the ball successfully.

12 You will hear two friends talking about a music festival they have been to.
They agree about

    A   the audience reaction.

    B   the variety of music.

    C   the fireworks

13 You will hear two friends talking about clothes for a party.
They agree that the boy should wear

    A   a suit and tie.

    B   a shirt and trousers.

    C   jeans and a T-shirt.

Turn over ▶

Part 3

Questions 14 – 19

For each question, write the correct answer in the gap. Write **one** or **two words** or a **number** or a **date** or a **time**.

You will hear a man called Eric Field telling a group of students about his work as journalist.

Being a journalist
Eric started writing about daily events when he was **(14)** ....
Eric says that journalists organise **(15)** .... into reports.
Eric thinks that a journalist must be willing to write about **(16)** ....
He or she must find a way to make the story **(17)** ....
A journalist must not change **(18)** ....
Eric thinks people should not get their news from **(19)** ....

Part 4

Questions 20 – 25

For each question, choose the correct answer.

You will hear a radio interview with a young woman called Joanna.

20 Joanna's hobby started making money

    A when she was a young child.
    B eighteen years ago.
    C very recently.

21 What is a new bird for Joanna?

    A one that hasn't been seen in that area
    B one that she hasn't seen before
    C one that no one has seen before

22 How many countries has Joanna been to?

    A 38
    B 20
    C half the countries in the world

23 Why didn't Joanna's blog become boring, according to her?

    A because she wrote about a lot of different countries
    B because she saw new birds each week because it
    C had photographs

24 Joanna will make money from her hobby

    A by selling her blog.
    B by selling advertising on her website.
    C by selling her life story in birdwatching.

25 How much will Joanna make when she signs a contract?

    A more than a quarter of a million pounds
    B a quarter of a million pounds
    C nearly a quarter of a million pounds

Cambridge B1 Preliminary

Listening

Test 8

© 2025 Prosperity Education.
'Cambridge B1 Preliminary' and 'PET' are brands belonging to The Chancellor, Masters and Scholars of the University of Cambridge and are not associated with Prosperity Education or its products.

Part 1

Questions 1 – 7

For each question, choose the correct answer.

1 What does the girl want to do at the weekend?

A

B

C

2 What did the boy have to eat at the restaurant last night?

A

B

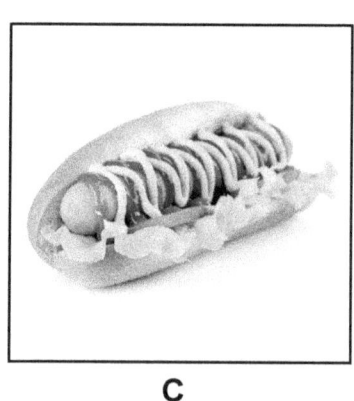
C

3 What must the students give the headteacher this week?

A

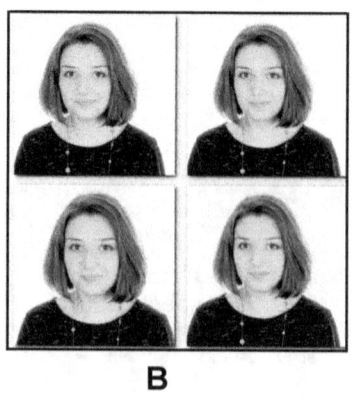
B

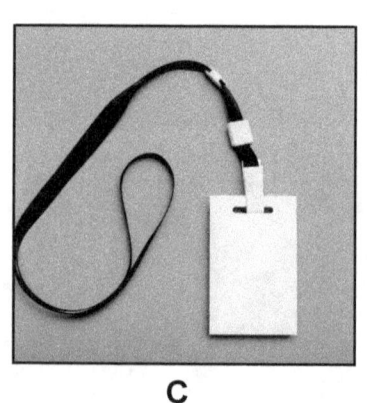
C

4 What was wrong at the girl's house?

A　　　　　　　　　　　B　　　　　　　　　　　C

5 How does the girl usually go home from school?

A　　　　　　　　　　　B　　　　　　　　　　　C

6 What did the girl like the most at the science fair?

A　　　　　　　　　　　B　　　　　　　　　　　C

7 Who is the boy seeing at the hospital?

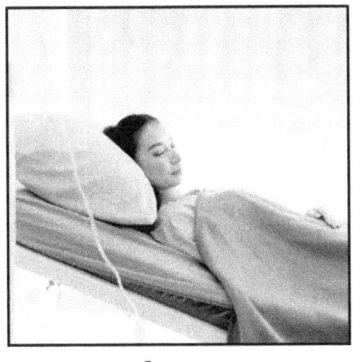  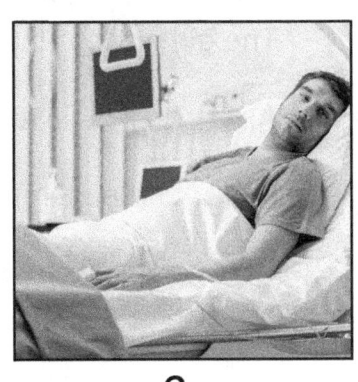

A　　　　　　　　　　　B　　　　　　　　　　　C

Turn over ▶

Part 2

Questions 8 – 13

For each question, choose the correct answer.

---

8   You will hear two friends talking about a film they have seen.
    What did the girl like about it?

   A   the music

   B   the photography

   C   the story

9   You will hear two friends talking about their school subjects.
    Which subject is the girl worried about?

   A   history

   B   maths

   C   science

10 You will hear a boy telling his friend about a shopping trip.
    What did he get?

   A   a jacket and trousers

   B   a jacket, trousers and a tie

   C   some T-shirts

11 You will hear two friends talking about a book for English literature.
    The girl advises the boy

   A   to give up reading the book.

   B   to read through the first hundred pages quickly.

   C   not to worry about the first hundred pages.

12 You will hear two friends talking about a concert they have been to.
They agree about

  A   the best song.

  B   the new songs.

  C   the volume of the music.

13 You will hear two friends talking about a tennis match.
They agree that

  A   the match was too long.

  B   one player was lucky.

  C   the match was exciting.

Turn over ▶

Part 3

Questions 14 – 19

For each question, write the correct answer in the gap. Write **one** or **two words** or a **number** or a **date** or a **time**.

You will hear a woman called Emma Thomas talking to a group of school students.

Being a fire officer
Emma left home at **(14)** ....
For a few weeks, Emma lived on **(15)** ....
Emma was helped by a man who asked her to **(16)** ....
She joined the fire service because she wanted to **(17)** ....
At first, Emma did not have a full-time job, but was **(18)** ....
Fire officers have to find the **(19)** .... of a fire

Part 4

Questions 20 – 25

For each question, choose the correct answer.

You will hear a radio interview with a nurse called Josh.

20 Josh's first nursing experience was

    A   looking after a pet rabbit.
    B   taking care of his father.
    C   nursing his mother at 12.

21 What is the name of Josh's job, according to him?

    A   nurse
    B   male nurse
    C   either 'nurse' or 'male nurse'

22 What does Josh think is the main reason for the small number of male nurses?

    A   Children see female nurses as dolls.
    B   Nurses on TV and in films are usually female.
    C   Parents don't want their sons to go into nursing.

23 What advantages does Josh see in being male in his job?

    A   He is stronger than most female nurses.
    B   There are no advantages.
    C   Some patients react better because he's male.

24 What disadvantages are there in him being male?

    A   It still surprises some people.
    B   There are none.
    C   He will be called 'Sister' after his promotion.

25 Josh never wanted to be a doctor because

    A   doctors have to learn so much.
    B   he isn't clever enough.
    C   he didn't want to make life or death decisions.

Cambridge B1 Preliminary

Listening

Test 9

Listening B1 | Ten tests for the Cambridge Preliminary

Part 1

Questions 1 – 7

For each question, choose the correct answer.

---

1 Where did the boy meet his friend yesterday?

A

B

C

2 How did the girl hurt her hand?

A

B

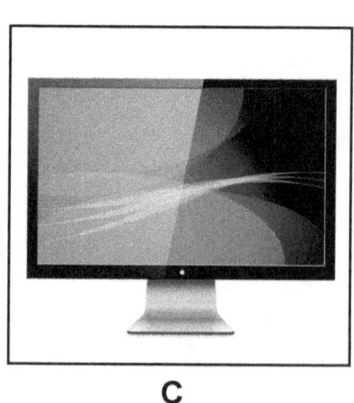
C

3 What must the students bring tomorrow?

A

B

C

4 Where was the dog found?

A

B

C

5 How does the girl usually get to school?

A

B

C

6 What is the subject of the poem which the girl likes best?

A

B

C

7 What is the boy going to play this afternoon?

A

B

C

Turn over ▶

Part 2

Questions 8 – 13

For each question, choose the correct answer.

8   You will hear two friends talking about a short story they have read.
    What didn't the girl like about it?

    A   the story

    B   the ending

    C   the length

9   You will hear two friends talking about part-time jobs.
    What is the girl's job?

    A   helping in her parents' shop

    B   delivering letters delivering

    C   newspapers

10 You will hear a boy telling his friend about a meal.
    What did he have to eat?

    A   fish and potatoes

    B   pasta

    C   pizza

11 You will hear two friends talking about a school test.
    The girl advises the boy

    A   to read all the chapters immediately.

    B   to do some revision every evening.

    C   to learn everything the night before.

12 You will hear two friends talking about learning an instrument.
They agree that

    A   it is boring to practise new things.

    B   the boy needs more lessons.

    C   the boy will never be as good as the girl.

13 You will hear two friends talking about clothes.
They agree about

    A   the colour of the boy's shirt.

    B   the prices in SupaStores.

    C   the clothes in SupaStores.

Turn over ▶

Part 3

Questions 14 – 19

For each question, write the correct answer in the gap. Write **one** or **two words** or a **number** or a **date** or a **time**.

You will hear a man called John Melville talking to a group of school students.

Choosing a good job
As a child, John's hobby was **(14)** ....
John got a Saturday morning job when he was **(15)** ....
John found the job **(16)** ....
John finished his degree course and then trained as a teacher for **(17)** .... year.
In his summer job as a language teacher, John earned £ **(18)** .... a week.
John says, 'You can't choose a good job. A good job **(19)** ....'

Part 4

Questions 20 – 25

For each question, choose the correct answer.

You will hear a radio interview with a young vet called Alice.

20 Alice learnt what she had to do to become a vet

    A   at the age of four.
    B   when one of her pets became ill.
    C   during a discussion at the riding school.

21 Why is maths important for vets?

    A   You have to work out how much medicine to give each animal.
    B   Animals have different heights and weights.
    C   Animals must be measured accurately.

22 What is the difference between Veterinary Science and Veterinary Medicine?

    A   Veterinary Science is only about treating sick animals.
    B   There is almost no difference between them
    C   Veterinary Medicine does not include how to diagnose animals.

23 What does Alice love about her job?

    A   It is well-paid.
    B   She gets a lot of free time.
    C   Every day is different.

24 How is Alice able to treat all the different kinds of animals?

    A   She needs to do regular research.
    B   Animals have the same basic body structure and way of working.
    C   Her university course taught her.

25 Alice advises students who want to be vets to

    A   work hard at school.
    B   work with animals as much as possible.
    C   choose the right subjects to study.

Cambridge B1 Preliminary

Listening

Test 10

© 2025 Prosperity Education.
'Cambridge B1 Preliminary' and 'PET' are brands belonging to The Chancellor, Masters and Scholars of the University of Cambridge and are not associated with Prosperity Education or its products.

Listening B1 | Ten tests for the Cambridge Preliminary

Part 1

Questions 1 – 7

For each question, choose the correct answer.

---

1 What does the girl usually do on Sunday afternoon?

A

B

C

2 What did the boy watch on television last night?

A

B

C

3 What will the children need first at the museum?

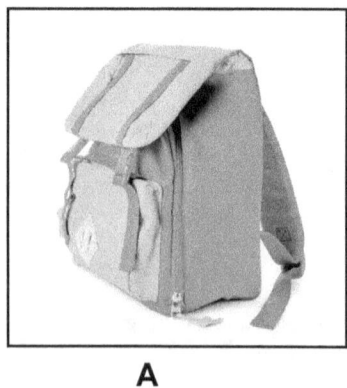
A

B

C

4 What will the weather be like on Friday?

A

B

C

5 Where does the girl have lunch on school days?

A

B

C

6 Which online learning site does the girl like best?

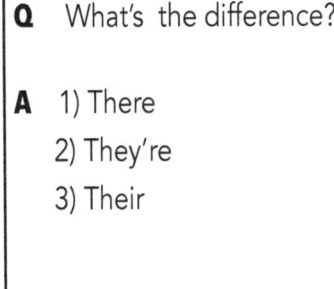
A

B

C

7 What's the matter with the boy's mother?

A

B

C

Turn over ▶

Part 2

Questions 8 – 13

For each question, choose the correct answer.

---

8   You will hear two friends talking about a film they have seen.
    What did the girl like best about it?

    A   the jokes

    B   the actors

    C   the story

9   You will hear two friends talking about their next holiday.
    What does the girl want to do?

    A   go on a cruise

    B   fly to a seaside hote

    C   go to a Caribbean beach

10 You will hear a boy telling his friend about a football match.
    What was the final score?

    A   2 - 0

    B   3 - 2

    C   2 - 2

11 You will hear two friends talking about the school play.
    The girl advises the boy

    A   to go through his long speech line by line.

    B   to take his time learning the speech.

    C   to make notes of the general points first.

12 You will hear two friends talking about their school uniform.
They agree that

    A   things will be better in Year 11.

    B   the boy's cap is nice.

    C   the school uniform is horrible.

13 You will hear two friends talking about a meal they've had.
They agree about

    A   the service.

    B   the cost.

    C   the quality of the food.

Turn over ▶

Part 3

Questions 14 – 19

For each question, write the correct answer in the gap. Write **one** or **two words** or a **number** or a **date** or a **time**.

You will hear a man called Karl Graham telling a group of students about his life as a comedy writer.

Being a comedy writer
Karl's talk is called, 'All jobs have **(14)** .... '.
Karl calls the first rule of comedy, 'the garden **(15)** .... '.
All good jokes have a set-up and a punch **(16)** .... which is not expected by the audience.
Karl sold his first jokes for £ **(17)** .... each.
Karl's second rule is, 'Know your **(18)** .... '.
Karl says, when people don't laugh at his jokes, it's not **(19)** ....

Part 4

Questions 20 – 25

For each question, choose the correct answer.

You will hear a radio interview with a young film star called Andi.

20 Andi thinks she became interested in acting

    A   at three.
    B   before she was five.
    C   after watching a film with a young girl in it.

21 What kind of film was Andi in first?

    A   a documentary about her school
    B   a police story for television
    C   an adventure story for the cinema

22 Why does Andi think she was chosen for the school film?

    A   because she was good at maths
    B   because she knew where her classroom was
    C   because she looked right

23 How did Andi get the part in her first proper film?

    A   She went to see an agent in London.
    B   An agent saw her in a school play.
    C   She flew to Hollywood

24 Where did she have to go for her first film?

    A   a hotel in London
    B   a film studio in the US
    C   a film studio in Londo

25 Andi finds it difficult to do

    A   the different parts.
    B   her schoolwork when she's filming.
    C   boring parts in films.

Answers

Practice Test 1: Listening Marking Key

Part 1 7 marks

1. A
2. B
3. C
4. B
5. C
6. A
7. C

Part 2 6 marks

8. C
9. B
10. A
11. C
12. A
13. B

Part 3 6 marks

14. 8 / eight
15. life / own life
16. play
17. 200
18. teacher
19. television / TV

Part 4 5 marks

20. B
21. A
22. C
23. B
24. A
25. C

Practice Test 2: Listening Marking Key

Part 1		7 marks
1	A	
2	C	
3	B	
4	A	
5	C	
6	A	
7	B	

Part 2		6 marks
8	C	
9	B	
10	C	
11	A	
12	B	
13	C	

Part 3		6 marks
14	animals	
15	6 / six	
16	subject	
17	5,000 / 5000	
18	rules	
19	weddings	

Part 4		5 marks
20	C	
21	A	
22	C	
23	B	
24	B	
25	C	

Practice Test 3: Listening Marking Key

Part 1   7 marks

1. A
2. C
3. A
4. B
5. C
6. A
7. B

Part 2   6 marks

8. B
9. A
10. B
11. C
12. A
13. C

Part 3   6 marks

14. 10/ten
15. rules
16. remind
17. stop worrying
18. learn
19. research

Part 4   5 marks

20. C
21. A
22. B
23. A
24. C
25. A

Practice Test 4: Listening Marking Key

Part 1		7 marks

1	B
2	A
3	C
4	A
5	B
6	C
7	B

Part 2		6 marks

8	C
9	B
10	C
11	A
12	C
13	B

Part 3		6 marks

14	12 / twelve
15	want
16	10 / ten
17	communication
18	organised
19	programs

Part 4		5 marks

20	B
21	A
22	C
23	A
24	B
25	C

Practice Test 5: Listening Marking Key

Part 1		7 marks
1	B	
2	A	
3	C	
4	A	
5	B	
6	C	
7	B	

Part 2		6 marks
8	C	
9	B	
10	A	
11	A	
12	C	
13	B	

Part 3		6 marks
14	12 / twelve	
15	his parents	
16	space	
17	want	
18	7 / seven	
19	materials	

Part 4		5 marks
20	C	
21	A	
22	C	
23	B	
24	A	
25	C	

Practice Test 6: Listening Marking Key

Part 1	7 marks
1	A
2	C
3	B
4	B
5	C
6	C
7	A

Part 2	6 marks
8	A
9	C
10	B
11	C
12	A
13	B

Part 3	6 marks
14	8/eight
15	maths
16	error
17	a company
18	progress
19	teachers

Part 4	5 marks
20	B
21	C
22	A
23	C
24	B
25	A

Practice Test 7: Listening Marking Key

Part 1   7 marks

1 C
2 B
3 A
4 C
5 A
6 A
7 C

Part 2   6 marks

8   B
9   A
10 B
11 C
12 A
13 B

Part 3   6 marks

14 6/six
15 events
16 everything/anything
17 interesting
18 the facts/the truth
19 social media

Part 4   5 marks

20 C
21 B
22 A
23 B
24 C
25 A

Practice Test 8: Listening Marking Key

Part 1		7 marks

1	B
2	C
3	A
4	B
5	A
6	C
7	B

Part 2		6 marks

8	B
9	A
10	C
11	C
12	A
13	B

Part 3		6 marks

14	15/fifteen
15	the streets
16	sell magazines
17	rescue people
18	on call
19	centre

Part 4		5 marks

20	C
21	A
22	A
23	B
24	A
25	C

Practice Test 9: Listening Marking Key

Part 1		7 marks
1	A	
2	C	
3	B	
4	A	
5	B	
6	C	
7	B	

Part 2		6 marks
8	C	
9	C	
10	A	
11	B	
12	A	
13	B	

Part 3		6 marks
14	maps	
15	14/fourteen	
16	boring	
17	one/1/a	
18	300	
19	chooses you	

Part 4		5 marks
20	C	
21	A	
22	B	
23	C	
24	A	
25	B	

Practice Test 10: Listening Marking Key

Part 1		7 marks
1	C	
2	A	
3	C	
4	B	
5	A	
6	C	
7	B	

Part 2		6 marks
8	C	
9	A	
10	B	
11	C	
12	A	
13	B	

Part 3		6 marks
14	rules	
15	path	
16	line	
17	50 / fifty	
18	audience	
19	funny	

Part 4		5 marks
20	B	
21	A	
22	C	
23	B	
24	C	
25	B	

Prosperity Education Ltd.
Cambridge, CB3 0HP
United Kingdom

Dear Customer,

Thank you for buying from us.

As an independent publisher, we would really appreciate it if you would leave us your honest feedback.

 Happy with your purchase? Simply log in to your Amazon account to leave a review.

 Not happy? Please reach out to our support team: admin@prosperityeducation.net

If you like our resources and what we do, please help us get our story out there.

 You can follow Prosperity Education (and in fact any of your favourite authors) on **Amazon**.

 Our **website** contains lots of free exam-practice materials and sample downloads.

 Our **Facebook** page regularly posts English language quizzes, discount codes and free stuff.

 Follow our **Instagram** stories for updates on our English teaching and learning resources.

 Subscribe to our **Youtube** channel for Listening, Speaking and Writing practice and tutorials.

I wish you all the very best for your studies.

Tom O'Reilly, Founder of Prosperity Education

PS. This resource is also available as **a PDF download** from www.prosperityeducation.net Enter the code 10PERCENTPDF at checkout for 10% off.

www.ingramcontent.com/pod-product-compliance
Lightning Source LLC
Chambersburg PA
CBHW081103070526
44584CB00021B/3185